Bible reflections
for older people

BRF

15 The Chambers, Vineyard
Abingdon OX14 3FE
brf.org.uk

Bible Reading Fellowship is a charity (233280)
and company limited by guarantee (301324),
registered in England and Wales

Acknowledgements

Scripture quotations marked with the following abbreviations are taken from the version shown. NRSV:
The New Revised Standard Version of the Bible, Anglicised edition, copyright © 1989, 1995 by the
Division of Christian Education of the National Council of the Churches of Christ in the United States
of America. Used by permission. All rights reserved. NIV: The Holy Bible, New International Version
(Anglicised edition) copyright © 1979, 1984, 2011 by Biblica. Used by permission of Hodder & Stoughton
Publishers, a Hachette UK company. All rights reserved. 'NIV' is a registered trademark of Biblica. UK
trademark number 1448790. CEV: the Contemporary English Version. New Testament © American
Bible Society 1991, 1992, 1995. Old Testament © American Bible Society 1995. Anglicisations © British
& Foreign Bible Society 1996. Used by permission. ESV: The Holy Bible, English Standard Version,
published by HarperCollins Publishers, © 2001 Crossway Bibles, a division of Good News Publishers.
Used by permission. All rights reserved. NKJV: the New King James Version®. Copyright © 1982 by
Thomas Nelson. Used by permission. All rights reserved. MSG: The Message, copyright © 1993, 1994,
1995, 1996, 2000, 2001, 2002 by Eugene H. Peterson. Used by permission of NavPress. All rights reserved.
Represented by Tyndale House Publishers, Inc. AMP: The Amplified® Bible (AMP), Copyright © 2015 by
The Lockman Foundation. Used by permission. www.Lockman.org. PHILLIPS: The New Testament in
Modern English by J.B Phillips copyright © 1960, 1972 J. B. Phillips. Administered by The Archbishops'
Council of the Church of England. Used by Permission. NLT: The Holy Bible, New Living Translation,
copyright © 1996, 2004, 2007, 2013. Used by permission of Tyndale House Publishers, Inc., Carol
Stream, Illinois 60188. All rights reserved. NLV: the New Life Version, copyright © 1969 and 2003. Used by
permission of Barbour Publishing, Inc., Uhrichsville, Ohio 44683. All rights reserved. GNT: the Good News
Bible published by The Bible Societies/HarperCollins Publishers Ltd, UK © American Bible Society 1966,
1971, 1976, 1992, used with permission.

A catalogue record for this book is available from the British Library

Printed and bound in the UK by Zenith Media NP4 0DQ

Contents

About the writers

Lynn Goslin was born in Edinburgh and brought up in the Scottish Episcopal Church. She completed her degree in linguistics and English language before training as a speech and language therapist. Her first marriage took her, as vicar's wife, to Canada for a few years and then to parishes in Norfolk and Yorkshire. She's a home group leader and ardent bell ringer at her church in North Yorkshire.

Martyn Payne worked with BRF for 15 years before retiring in 2017. His last role was Messy Church researcher. He has a background in Bible storytelling and leading all-age worship and is passionate about the blessing that comes from intergenerational worship. For the past three years, he has been BRF's volunteer prayer advocate, writing prayers for social media and putting together the BRF prayer diary.

Lin Ball's career began in journalism over 40 years ago. She delights in the variety of work that has come her way: ghost-written books, magazine articles about missionary work, communications for Christian charities and radio interviews on disability. She spent twelve years as Bible resources editor with Scripture Union. Lin lives in the east Midlands, where she still writes, is active in eco-groups in her market town and enjoys long walks.

Roger Combes has served in a variety of parishes in London, Cambridge and Hastings. Before retiring he was archdeacon of Horsham. He and his wife, Christine, now live in Crawley, West Sussex, where Christine is the gardener and he cuts the grass.

From the Editor

Welcome.

I love the idea of 'proper' paper maps, but on a wet and windy moor, reading faint brown contour lines through foggy varifocals is a challenge, so I'm a recent convert to GPS devices. It took persistence to master the technology, but the effort paid off when I walked St Oswald's Way last autumn. For much of the route, there was 'no visible path'. Without my new best friend, Garmin, I might still be lost in Harewood Forest.

The device bleeped when I was on course and helped me find my way back when I had strayed. It was a rare and quietly awesome experience to be alone in a landscape for hours and miles on end; it would have been daunting without the gadget in my hand.

Feeling lost, physically and spiritually, can be terrifying. But if we can resist panic in the midst of disorientation, we can learn new ways of thinking and being; we discover new depths of confidence both in our own resilience and in our trust in the constancy of God and the new paths he opens up before us.

Approaching Holy Island, at the end of St Oswald's Way, the so-called pilgrim's path is washed away twice a day. A line of slender marker posts shows the route across the wet sand at low tide, as powerfully symbolic of God's guiding hand as the bleep of my GPS device.

God bless you.

Eley
x

Using these reflections

Perhaps you have always had a special time each day for reading the Bible and praying. But now, as you grow older, you are finding it more difficult to keep to a regular pattern or find it harder to concentrate. Or, maybe you've never done this before. Whatever your situation, these Bible reflections aim to help you take a few moments to read God's word and pray whenever you have time or feel that would be helpful.

When to read them

You might use these Bible reflections in the morning or last thing at night, but they work at any time of day. There are 40 reflections here, grouped around four themes, by four different writers. Each one includes some verses from the Bible, a reflection to help you in your own thinking about God, and a prayer suggestion. The reflections aren't dated, so it doesn't matter if you don't want to read every day. The Bible verses are printed, but you might prefer to follow them in your own Bible.

How to read them

- **Take time** to quieten yourself, becoming aware of God's presence, asking him to speak to you through the Bible and the reflection.

- **Read** the Bible verses and the reflection:
  - What do you especially like or find helpful in these verses?
  - What might God be saying to you through this reading?
  - Is there something to pray about or thank God for?

- **Pray.** Each reflection includes a prayer suggestion. You might like to pray for yourself or take the opportunity to think about and pray for others.

Do not be afraid

Lynn Goslin

What would it be like to live without fear? It's difficult to imagine when 24-hour news broadcasts and social media bring us reports of wars and rumours of wars, of national disasters and individual tragedies.

Our circumstances may produce fear: of poverty, homelessness, loneliness, collapse of relationships, illness, death.

Even our faith can bring fear: perhaps the deep-seated fear of an early (mis)understanding of God as a God of impossible rules, of judgement and wrath. Or perhaps our own lack of self-esteem and self-worth results in fear: we feel only failure and unworthiness, believing ourselves to be unacceptable and unlovable.

I am always struck by the assurance and reassurance of the 'Comfortable Words' in the Book of Common Prayer service of Holy Communion. Again and again, in challenging situations in both Old and New Testaments, people are told not to be afraid and are given encouragement to persevere. This series explores some of those occasions so that we too might look past our fear and be comforted and encouraged.

Isaiah 43:1b (NRSV)

Called by name

Do not fear, for I have redeemed you; I have called you by name, you are mine.

In many cultures knowing someone's name gives power. To be called by name can have negative connotations: you can be summoned; be discussed in your absence; be called out for bad behaviour; be identified as the person responsible.

On the other hand, your name said by a family member or friend instantly brings you and all that you are into the hearer's mind. In a family, a nickname or diminutive of your name identifies you as a treasured and loved part of the group.

In this verse from Isaiah, God first assures you – 'Do not fear' – then he calls you. This is not a summoning by the great headmaster in the sky, nor a suggestion that you belong to him as property. Rather, it is a loving call to one who is, as the metaphors have it, one of his flock, a branch of his vine and, loveliest of all, one of his children, identified as having his likeness upon you and known intimately to him by your own name. So hear his call and do not fear.

■ PRAYER

Father of love, thank you that you know my name and know all that I am. Help me not to let fear stop me from answering your loving call. Amen

Isaiah 41:9b–10 (NRSV, abridged)

Chosen

I have chosen you and not cast you off; do not fear, for I am with you… I will strengthen you, I will help you.

Sorting out my overstuffed wardrobe involves conceding that choices I made while shopping have not always been good ones, and many clothes deservedly end up being cast off.

When Jesus chose his disciples, he made some odd choices: fishermen, a tax collector, a zealot. Fortunately, as Isaiah makes clear, God's choices do not get cast off as easily as clothing. When Peter hears Jesus say that his friends will leave him at the final moment, he declares unwavering faithfulness, only to then hear Jesus' prediction of his three-times denial. His utter desolation when he realises that he has done precisely as Jesus predicted is one of the most heartrending moments of the passion story. We have all been there, looking at Jesus and knowing that we have failed him yet again.

But we continue to be chosen. At the empty tomb, an angel sends a message of hope to the disciples 'and Peter' (Mark 16:7). What a cheering and encouraging message, assuring Peter that he was still chosen, loved and part of God's plans. Even after total failure, the promise stands for us as well: 'I will strengthen you, I will help you.'

■ PRAYER

Lord, help me to rejoice in the knowledge that I am chosen as I am. Strengthen me and help me in times of failure. Amen

Psalm 121:8 (NRSV)

Going out and coming in

The Lord will keep your going out and your coming in from this time on and forevermore.

A Franciscan friend was once asked if she had met a well-known preacher visiting their house. 'No,' she said. 'I was on washing-up duty that day; all I heard were peals of laughter coming down the corridor!'

Everyday routines can give us the spiritual version of FOMO: fear of missing out. We feel we could be exploring a more heightened, intense experience of God. Our daily activities can be just boring, or truly a grind, crushing our spirit into dullness or even depression.

The long tradition of practising the presence of God chimes with centuries-old Celtic prayers used to welcome God into each action of the day – lighting a fire, milking cows, crossing the threshold. God is present in 'your going out and your coming in', the most ordinary of activities.

This is not the baleful eye of God as usually depicted in old wall-hangings but the interested and loving gaze of a parent for a beloved child. He is here now, 'from this time on' – let us welcome his presence in to make the ordinary extraordinary.

■ PRAYER

Lord, in the ordinary moments of today, let me know your loving presence. Amen

Luke 5:8b, 10b (NRSV)

Go away

[Simon Peter said,] 'Go away from me, Lord, for I am a sinful man!'... Jesus said to Simon, 'Do not be afraid; from now on you will be catching people.'

As a teenager, I was both thrilled and dismayed by the stories missionaries working abroad brought back to our church. Thrilled because it was amazing to hear of their adventures and incredible work; dismayed because I was afraid God would call me to a similar task, which I felt unequal to and unfitted for.

Peter has been overwhelmed by a revelation of Jesus' nature and power. In contrast, he sees himself in all his failure as a sinful man and asks Jesus to go away, imagining that he, Peter, is unworthy and useless to this dazzling Lord.

Jesus' response is to reassure him – Peter's fear is unnecessary. Not only is he accepted as he is, but he is given a calling eminently suited to him because Jesus knows him better than he knows himself – remember the cock crowing!

Seeing ourselves clearly in the light that Jesus brings can be daunting. But Jesus does not allow Peter to dwell unhealthily on his shortcomings: he has a part to play in God's kingdom. As with Peter, our dismay at our failures is the first step to finding out what Jesus is actually asking us to do.

■ **PRAYER**

Lord, help me to know myself, yet face you without fear. Make my path straight on the way that you have asked me to go. Amen

Mark 6:50–51a (NRSV)

Take heart

[Jesus said,] 'Take heart, it is I; do not be afraid.' Then he got into the boat.

My friend's birthday card had a picture on it of a mountaineer reaching the summit. The speech bubble read, 'Now, what did I come up here for?' We both laughed because of our shared experience of increasing forgetfulness.

We talk about 'being in the same boat' as someone else when we share a human experience or deep emotion: the joy at a grandchild's first steps, relief as a friend comes out of hospital, anxiety over money or moving house.

Jesus' complete humanity allows him to utter the right words: firstly, the calming of the heart; secondly, the engagement of the intellect. 'It is I', the most comforting thing he could have said. 'Do not be afraid' becomes possible because trust is no longer overcome by fear.

In Rumer Godden's book, *In This House of Brede* (Macmillan, 1969), a troubled character finds that 'the broken knees of the figure on the crucifix comforted her; he had known what it was to fall... Christ, God made man, was human.' The incarnation is assurance that God knows what it is like to be us. In the metaphorical sense, and for the disciples at that moment in reality, Jesus was and is in the same boat as us. Let us take heart.

■ **PRAYER**

Lord my boat sails in difficult waters. Stand with me and help me to take heart. Amen

1 John 4:18–19 (NRSV, abridged)

Perfect love casts out fear

Perfect love casts out fear; for fear has to do with punishment… We love because he first loved us.

One of my primary school friends constructed an elaborate story about teddy bear thieves to disguise the fact that she had 'borrowed' another girl's teddy bear after a sleepover. The story did not fool the adults, the bear was duly returned and the wee girl suitably admonished.

We often fool ourselves with the deceptions we spin to put off confronting our own shortcomings. Understandable, because with confrontation comes the old expectation of judgement and punishment, often born from experiences in our early life.

Visiting a hospice patient, a friend found the lady frightened, not of dying, but of judgement. Together they shared Psalm 139:1: 'O Lord, you have searched me and known me.' God has already been intimately involved in every aspect of our lives, even the ones we would like to hide from him and ourselves. The judgement, in a sense, has already been made; he knows our shortcomings and shame, and his perfect love of us, just as we are, continues to embrace us, encompassing our past, our present and our future.

■ **PRAYER**

Lord, you know all my fears. Allow me to know all your love. Amen

Psalm 23:4a (NRSV)

Going home

Even though I walk through the darkest valley, I fear no evil; for you are with me.

However refreshing and enjoyable a holiday has been, coming home is often a comforting and joyful experience. 'I want to go home!' is the distressed child's expression of the desire we all have at some time to be enfolded in the familiar, the known, the safe place.

Not everyone has experienced a loving home life, yet all of us have had that longing to be held in a place of total acceptance, understanding, compassion and love, which we see as the true nature of going home. Augustine rightly says, 'Our hearts are restless until they rest in you.' We want to go home.

'Going home' is an old metaphor for dying. The 'darkest valley' is sometimes rendered as 'the valley of the shadow of death'. The psalmist senses God's presence with him in life – 'you are with me' – but we also know Paul's great declaration: 'I am convinced that neither death nor life... will be able to separate us from the love of God in Christ Jesus our Lord' (Romans 8:38–39). In the parable of the prodigal son, the father eagerly rushes to embrace his son; Jesus is depicting for us his Father's welcome as we come home to him.

■ **PRAYER**
Lord, fulfil my heart's longing to be at home with you now, and in the long home of your eternal love. Amen

Deuteronomy 7:18a (NRSV)

Just remember

Do not be afraid of them. Just remember what the Lord your God did.

Reading through the Old Testament it seems as though the early Israelites were always setting up stones as memorials to significant encounters with God. And then, of course, moving on to forget them and make the same mistakes again.

The same is true in my life: not that I set up memorial stones in this literate age but looking back over diaries and journals I find that I have wrestled with the same fears and worries in repeating patterns over the years. However, looking back gives perspective: that fear, tied to a particular past event, turned out to be groundless; this fear was justified and had to be faced, but was resolved – or, at least, I survived and moved on.

The trouble is 'just remembering'. A friend was once tempted to throw out her spiritual journal – 'self-absorbed wittering', she declared – and I understood from my own jottings what she meant. Unlike the Israelites, we forget to put down a marker stone; we record our fears but not God's action. But the truth is, if I use them to record what God has done in my life and what he has promised he will do, then my diaries *are* a reminder of God's faithful love and companionship as I navigate the ups and downs of life.

■ **PRAYER**

Lord, in my present fears remind me of all you have done, and strengthen me. Amen

John 14:27 (NRSV, abridged)

My peace I give to you

[Jesus said,] 'My peace I give to you... Do not let your hearts be troubled and do not let them be afraid.'

As a champion worrier, I know I cannot 'add a single hour to [my] span of life' (Luke 12:25) by worrying, but the habit of being 'troubled' continues. I worry about the past – *Was that the right decision? What did they think of me?* I worry about the future – *What shall I wear? Will I have enough money?*

Some 'worries' constitute sensible reflection. We need to revisit past events to learn from and perhaps change our behaviour or response. Similarly, it is not worrying to plan for the future: dates on the calendar, shopping lists, holidays.

Problems arise when our hearts are preoccupied with things that are not the unfailing treasures of heaven (Luke 12:33–34). A friend asked me to imagine a life where no one judged appearance, clothes, ability and so on. I was overwhelmed, imagining the relief and freedom as lifelong worries dropped away. All that lost time and wasted energy recovered.

Worry is usually about the past or the future, but it makes our hearts troubled in the present, constricting our ability to live freely. Jesus offers an exchange – of his peace for a troubled heart – so we can present ourselves as a living sacrifice (Romans 12:1) instead of battling to present ourselves to the world.

■ **PRAYER**

Lord, my heart is often troubled; let me accept your peace. Amen

Isaiah 41:13 (NRSV)

I will help you

For I, the Lord your God, hold your right hand; it is I who say to you, 'Do not fear, I will help you.'

On a radio programme I listened to, someone explained that they had conquered their fear of heights by learning to skydive. An extreme example of facing your fears but it highlights the courage we need to look honestly at what causes us to fear – making us vulnerable, prey to feelings of failure, anxiety, and even anger and jealousy at others who seem strong when we feel weak.

Paul understood the paradox that it is our very weakness that, when we hit rock bottom, allows us to be in the best position to rely entirely on God's strength. God had said to him, 'My grace is sufficient for you, for power is made perfect in weakness' (2 Corinthians 12:9).

The picture of God in Isaiah holding us by our right hand is a powerful one. It conjures up an image of one who knows the way leading one who is uncertain, or of a parent taking a child's hand to guide and keep them safe. This is the God whose grace is sufficient, who runs towards the needy prodigal and welcomes them in, who is acquainted with all their ways (Psalm 139:3). This is the God who, as Paul says, 'is able to accomplish abundantly far more than all we can ask or imagine' (Ephesians 3:20).

■ **PRAYER**

Lord, in my weakness and in your generous love, hold my right hand. Amen

Think about these things

Martyn Payne

'Finally... whatever is true... noble... right... pure... lovely... admirable – if anything is excellent or praiseworthy – think about such things. Whatever you have learned or received or heard from me, or seen in me – put it into practice. And the God of peace will be with you' (Philippians 4:8–9, NIV).

There is no shortage today of suggested remedies for our anxieties. There are music meditation podcasts, mindfulness guides, breathing exercises and online courses, all of which 'guarantee' peace of mind. And, of course, there is no doubt that life has become increasingly complex and difficult to navigate nowadays, so the offer of possible ways to cope is understandably very attractive.

But life was not without its challenges in the past too, when the followers of Jesus read Paul's wise advice as recorded in these verses from Philippians. What we focus on can have a profound influence on the way we are and how we manage the ups and downs of everyday life. In these few words, Paul offers us a simple recipe for a Christ-centred mindfulness that can lead to God's peace, described earlier in this chapter as that which 'transcends all understanding' (v. 7).

The following reflections explore the Bible's solution to the stresses and strains of life. It isn't an expensive course you have to buy or an app you must download, but wonderfully it is freely available to us all through the grace of God in Jesus Christ. Paul is signposting the way to the peace of God, 'which will guard your hearts and your minds in Christ Jesus' (v. 7). How might we begin to put Paul's advice into practice in the days to come?

1 Timothy 1:15 (CEV)

Whatever is true

'Christ Jesus came into the world to save sinners.' This saying is true, and it can be trusted. I was the worst sinner of all!

It's becoming increasingly hard to find the truth about a situation nowadays. What is claimed to be true is too often merely opinion, social media comment, 'clever' interpretation of statistics or, in times of war and political change, propaganda. So where do we go to find truth and how can we know it is trustworthy?

Jesus claimed to be the truth and frequently prefaced his sayings with the phrase, 'Truly, truly, I say to you.' Truth is not relative; it is absolute and found in God alone. And God's truth is made visible in Christ, who stepped into our world to show us truth in action. This can rescue us all from the lies that are told to us, the lies we tell others and even the lies we tell ourselves. In the presence of God's truth, our confusion about what is true is exposed. Yet take heart, because God sent Jesus to save us from exactly that confusion.

Today's verse is a truth worth meditating on every day. One that reminds us of how much God loves us and what it cost to rescue us, which in turn gives us the hope of discovering who we are truly meant to be.

■ **PRAYER**
Thank you for the certain truth that God sent Jesus to rescue me, even though I don't deserve it, in any way at all. Amen

Proverbs 3:9 (CEV)

Whatever is honourable

Honour the Lord by giving him your money and the first part of all your crops.

Among the many honourable actions that are recommended throughout the Bible, this advice from Proverbs is immensely practical and can contribute more to our peace of mind than we might imagine.

Money worries are often cited as the cause of much mental ill health. The fear of not being able to pay the monthly household bills or put food on the table is a serious issue and is a matter of real concern for many families in our increasingly divided society. Bible injunctions, such as 'Do not worry' and 'Do not fear', can sound hollow and fail to bring comfort when the debts are mounting. So what hope is there for peace of mind in situations like this?

According to this verse, the honourable action here is firstly to rethink our understanding of money, which, however little or much that is, is God's not ours; and secondly, not to give up the regular habit of giving away a percentage to others who are in even greater need. This approach can help break the control that money has over our minds and hearts. It can lead to a peace that surpasses understanding and to an experience of God's provision that is always just enough for the day ahead.

■ PRAYER

May I never forget that all that I have comes from you and it is always of your own that I give back to you. Amen

Genesis 18:25 (CEV)

Whatever is right

'You are the judge of all the earth, and you do what is right.'

When we read that God created us 'in his own image' (Genesis 1:27, NIV), surely one of the characteristics we inherit is a sense of justice – a deep awareness of right and wrong. It should be no surprise that the presence of injustice in this world disturbs most of us and inspires a longing that things should be put right.

Abraham wrestled with questions like this when he talked with God about the fate of Sodom and Gomorrah, which is the context for the verse above. However, he was not arguing that people should not be punished but rather that innocent people should not suffer. There is no doubt that such things do trouble us, and the more we know, the more disturbed we can be. So where do we find peace of mind in this instance?

The answer is in the same place that Abraham found it, namely in a faith that God will always do the right thing. God sees the whole picture and the best outcome. Moreover God also knows first-hand what injustice feels like, having experienced it in the life and death of Jesus Christ. Learning to rest in the confidence that God will always be fair and just and do the right thing can help us find peace among the many storms of this life.

■ **PRAYER**

Lord, help me to trust in you as the God of justice, who will always do the right thing. Amen

Psalm 12:6 (ESV)

Whatever is pure

The words of the Lord are pure words, like silver refined in a furnace on the ground, purified seven times.

We value things that are pure: from pure gold to pure water. We stay clear of things that are contaminated. There is already so much out there that has tainted our lives that we long for what is pure.

When it comes to finding inner peace, reading or listening to the pure words of God is one of the best things we can do. The prophet Habakkuk wrote that God is so pure that he cannot even look upon evil (Habakkuk 1:13). God's pure words are all about bringing us good, even when they rebuke, correct or redirect us in some way.

In some parts of scripture, we become particularly aware of the purifying effect of God's words. These are usually found when God speaks peace into a situation, or where the psalmist becomes very aware of the closeness of God. And of course there are the precious words of Jesus, particularly when he welcomes the stranger, the sinner and the sinned-against.

Too often we allow ourselves to be shaped and defined by what others say of us, rather by than the pure words of God which can transform us into the best we can be. Which of God's words are like pure water to your soul?

■ PRAYER

God says to you: I made you, I have chosen you, I have kept you, I have redeemed you and I love you. Amen

Psalm 96:9a (NKJV)

Whatever is lovely

Oh, worship the Lord in the beauty of holiness!

This verse has been painted on to a board which is mounted on the wall of the little church where I worship in Essex. Great care was taken to colour the calligraphy lettering so that it is something lovely for worshippers to look at. It is a thing of beauty while also reminding us that holiness itself is a beautiful thing that invites us into a place of peace.

Sadly the word 'holiness' is too often misunderstood in today's world. It has come to mean pious, remote and other-worldly. For many it conjures up pictures of saints with their halos from long ago, who seem very far removed from ordinary people. But this is not Christian holiness. God's holiness is something beautiful, lovely and attractive; those who share in God's character through the work of the Holy Spirit can radiate such holiness.

I pray there are people like this who you know, who draw you into a beautiful holiness that is from God, inspiring your worship of the Lord and the experience of God's peace. And in turn, although I'm sure you won't acknowledge it, people will see that same loveliness in you, so that you will be helping them on that same journey.

■ **PRAYER**

Holy God, open my eyes to your holiness shining out of the people that I will meet this day, and help me through my life to inspire others to worship you. Amen

Luke 4:22 (ESV)

Whatever is gracious

All spoke well of [Jesus] and marvelled at the gracious words that were coming from his mouth.

In his gospel, John describes the Word made flesh as being 'full of grace' (John 1:14). Jesus is the personification of grace. But 'grace' is not a word that we hear that much today. So what do 'grace' and 'gracious' signify, and how might this address our anxieties and lead us into God's peace?

Many have attempted to define this very precious Christian word. Grace is something undeserved and unexpected; it is the experience of God's love that Christians enjoy, as they put their trust in Jesus; it is the blessing of God that comes as we welcome God's presence into our lives. The words of Jesus, as remembered and recorded for us by his followers in the gospels, open the door to this grace, which enriches, affirms and reorientates our lives towards all that is good and true.

At the heart of our faith sit the sayings of Jesus and the more we get to know what he said, the more our soul is rooted in God's peace. Filling our minds with what Jesus said is one of the best ways to banish all our anxieties and fears.

■ PRAYER

Call to mind some of the words of Jesus that you remember, and spend time now repeating them slowly so they become part of your day and an anchor for whatever lies ahead.

1 Corinthians 12:31 (ESV)

Whatever is excellent

But earnestly desire the higher gifts. And I will show you a still more excellent way.

With this verse Paul introduces one of the most well-known and beautiful poems in the New Testament. What follows in chapter 13 is a hymn to love, naming and celebrating its many beautiful characteristics. This is the 'excellent way' that Paul is talking about – the excellent way of love.

God is love and God has poured that love not only into us his children but also into every aspect of the created order. Love is waiting to be experienced and found in nature and in everything that lives and breathes. It's a love that is found not just among our Christian brothers and sisters, but is also very much at work in many surprising people and unexpected places.

Focusing our minds on love, wherever we can find it, can be truly life-bringing and so vital for our inner well-being. Opening our hearts to that love, wherever we find it, can bring healing to our anxious minds. Sadly the stories of such love are too often buried beneath the bad news of our times, but they are there, if we will but look out for them each day. They are waiting to become part of our journey into God's peace.

■ **PRAYER**

God of love, help me to become more alert to your love at work this day, in all people, in all places and at all times. Amen

Revelation 19:5 (ESV)

Whatever is praiseworthy

And from the throne came a voice saying, 'Praise our God, all you his servants, you who fear him, small and great.'

When it comes to thinking about 'whatever is praiseworthy', surely the events of Good Friday to Easter Sunday are the best encouragement for praise ever. And if you want one book of the Bible that is full of more praise than any other, Revelation is the place to turn.

The chapters of this last book of the Bible are full of worship songs, and many of them particularly reference 'the Lamb that was slain'. It seems that heaven itself forever echoes with wonder at what happened at Calvary.

However, for some of us maybe, this supremely praiseworthy event has become dulled through repetition and familiarity. This is a shame, because once we refocus our attention on this pivotal truth of our faith, we get our lives in perspective; and whatever is burdening us, in mind or in spirit, can be enveloped in the unchanging peace of God. Indeed, this is why God invites us to join in with the praise of heaven.

Praise by its very nature turns us outward and away from harmful introspection. God doesn't need our praises, but God knows that celebrating what is worthy of praise is for our good.

■ **PRAYER**

Call to mind the old chorus, 'Turn your eyes upon Jesus'. Sing this to yourself today to help you focus on Jesus and God's love.

Isaiah 26:3 (ESV)

Think about these things

You keep him in perfect peace whose mind is stayed on you, because he trusts in you.

We may have come to the end of Paul's list of good things on which to focus our hearts and minds, but if we then do nothing about it, we will have missed Paul's message. He wants us to take time to reflect on these words. So how do we keep our mind 'stayed on God', as Isaiah advises? Maybe it has something to do with relearning the art of prayer.

For too many of us prayer has become dominated by intercession. It's understandable, because there's so much to pray for and so many needs in the world. But God knows this, and of course it is these very needs that drive us to prayer. However, prayer is much more than just asking for something for ourselves or others. Prayer is about opening up our hearts and minds to God's love and, in God's intimate presence, allowing God to fill us with truth, honour, justice, purity, beauty, grace, praise and all things excellent.

Only when these things are primary, shaping our thinking and then our words, can we begin to experience the true purpose of prayer, which, remarkably, is not so much about changing other people and situations, but is first and foremost about changing us.

■ PRAYER

Here I am, Lord, not asking for things for others nor even for myself, but simply asking for you. Amen

2 Thessalonians 3:16a (ESV)

And the God of peace will be with you

Now may the Lord of peace himself give you peace at all times in every way.

In his letters to the churches, Paul often includes references to the peace of God. Indeed peace lies at the heart of the good news: it is through Jesus that we have peace with God; and Jesus is the peace that brings together people who were once enemies.

It is peace that we all long for, both for ourselves and for those who are caught in the troubles of this world. Paul believed that God's peace was powerful and effective enough to meet even the most disturbed situations people may find themselves in. His readers did not live easy lives. Many worked as slaves and were subject to brutality and injustice; others faced persecution and prejudice; and all lived precarious lives in a world with wars, diseases and limited life expectancy. And yet in these very circumstances, the gospel offered them the precious gift of God's peace.

This is the same peace as that which followed the storm on the lake and that which restored a deranged man to his right mind. It was Jesus, the Prince of Peace, who brought peace to these situations, and that same peace is available for each of us, whatever we face this day.

■ PRAYER

Turn these words of Jesus into a prayer for yourself: 'Peace I leave with you; my peace I give to you' (John 14:27).

The Gift of Years

 Debbie Thrower is the pioneer of BRF's Anna Chaplaincy for Older People ministry, offering spiritual care to older people, and is widely involved in training and advocacy.

Visit **annachaplaincy.org.uk** to find out more.

Debbie writes...

Welcome!

Martyn Payne has chosen one of my favourite Bible passages to focus on in this issue. It's from Philippians, so, as the old Collect goes, 'mark, learn and inwardly digest':

'Whatever is true, whatever is honourable, whatever is just, whatever is pure, whatever is lovely, whatever is commendable, if there is any excellence, if there is anything worthy of praise, think about these things' (Philippians 4:8, ESV).

It is wise advice Paul dispenses here. Cognitive behavioural therapy helps people to manage problems by changing the way they think and behave. In a similar vein, by reading the Bible, exposing ourselves to what is positive and truthful, we can reframe our perspective.

In his letter to the Philippians, Paul's urging to concentrate on what is honourable, pure, pleasing and commendable is not just wishful thinking. It is a vital tool for resilience, for combatting thoughts and images which can drag us down.

I hope you'll find much in these pages to 'think about', be encouraged by and to buoy you up.

Best wishes

Debbie

Meet Lynn Goslin

 Lynn Goslin was born and rasied in Edinburgh. She went to St Thomas', Corstorphine, an evangelical Episcopalian church, though her life since then has embraced many other church experiences, from charismatic to Anglo-Catholic with contemplative prayer. After a degree in English language and linguistics at the University of Edinburgh, Lynn did a further qualification in speech and language therapy and went to work in Glasgow. But by that point, she'd met the man who was to be her husband, who was training to be a vicar. Lynn takes up the story:

'I married Roger and he had taken a job in the Yukon, Canada, so I ended up in a church just off a First Nations reservation and spent four rather cold but interesting and challenging years there, which was lovely in lots of ways. Although we were in the diocese of Yukon, we were actually in northern British Columbia, which is a little bit more springlike than further north. But we did get to travel into the Arctic Circle, and I did experience temperatures of minus 44, which is the coldest I've ever known. But I think we both were a bit homesick and so were glad to take a parish in Norfolk.'

Lynn enjoyed rural life in England, and Norfolk was followed by North Yorkshire, where she had two daughters and worked as a speech and language therapist. 'Life was good,' she says, 'but it didn't last and our marriage broke down.' She stayed in the area but changed churches, moving to a church in Kirkbymoorside in 1997, where she has been ever since. 'They were terrific! They looked after the children and they looked after me, and as I got stronger again, I worked full-time during the week and became a junior church leader at the weekends, and I went on the PCC. And now I bell-ring. I've even started ringing for the service on Sunday morning, now that I'm no longer running junior church.'

Lynn got to know about BRF three or four years ago, when her church decided to form home groups. 'The first set of materials we used really did not go down well, and we were in danger of having a revolution on our hands. It so happens that Sr Helen Julian, one of BRF's authors and a regular contributor to BRF Bible reading notes, was a very, very long-standing friend of mine. Very sadly, she died in 2021.'

Lynn continues: 'We'd gone to school together in Edinburgh from the age of five. I had two or three good friends, but Helen was the only one that I could talk to about church and spiritual things. So when we were looking for new materials for the groups, I asked Helen if she could recommend anything, and she said how about chatting to BRF? We settled on Holy Habits, which Helen had written for. That was really the turning point for the groups, I would say.'

Lynn shared the story of her home groups with us, and it's posted on **holyhabits.org.uk** (click 'community', then 'stories'). Having got to know her a bit, we thought she might have hidden talents as a writer.

So it has proved and we can now all enjoy her first series for *Bible Reflections for Older People,* called 'Do not be afraid'. But what brought her to this point?

'My life has been spent writing patients' reports, in which you have to be concise and clear, so I suppose I've spent my life writing. I've always liked writing. Like Helen Julian, I've tried my hand at poetry and stuff, but I've never published anything and often thought that perhaps I could go that way. When I left work three years ago, one of the girls gave me a notebook and she said, "I love your stories. Write them down."'

So what was the inspiration for this series?

'My own fears, actually. Particularly in lockdown, having a lot of time to think and seeing other people's anxieties. I'm a great one for thinking that if you can face your fear and understand it, you're part of the way to conquering it yourself. But there are some fears that you can't easily conquer yourself: they need the love of God, and to be able to rest in him. He knows our fear. I really wanted to write something consoling and hopeful. I hope that's what people take away from the reflections.'

Believing beyond the dark...

Our poem in this issue is by an Australian sister, Raphael Consedine PBVM, who died in 2000. She was known as a gifted poet, storyteller, historian and teacher. She travelled nationally and internationally – to Papua New Guinea, Africa, the United States, Ireland and New Zealand, sharing the story of her community, the Presentation Sisters Victoria, and offering retreats. In 2001, her sisters published a collection of her poems, entitled *Songs of the Journey*, which has been widely shared and warmly received. *Songs of the Journey* is available (£3.00 plus p&p) from Presentation Sisters Victoria, PO Box 2276, St Kilda West, Victoria, Australia 3182; or email **admin@presvic.org.au**.

Presentation... and the child danced before the Lord

In the morning of your life, Mary
you danced before the Lord.
Later on, much later on,
you stood still in his presence
through a long darkness.

Mary, steadfast one,
grant that when we can no longer dance
we may stand beside you,
still, in God's presence,
believing beyond the dark.

'Presentation… and the child danced before the Lord' from *Songs of the Journey* by Raphael Consedine (Presentation Sisters Victoria, 2001), used by permission of Presentation Sisters Victoria.

Meet Jane Bull

Shortly after she celebrated her 99th birthday in February 2022, Jane Bull wrote to BRF, in part to voice her appreciation of *Bible Reflections for Older People* and our commitment to 'bringing the faith to people of all ages' and in part to volunteer her help.

Jane's family moved to the village of Shalfleet on the Isle of Wight in 1935 and immediately became involved in St Michael the Archangel Church in Shalfleet. When she was old enough, Jane joined the Sunday school and the choir and was confirmed at the age of 14. She has lived much of her life on the island, apart from a time working in Salisbury after she left school and when she served in the Women's Auxiliary Air Force during World War II. After the war, she trained as a primary school teacher, with RE as her main subject.

Jane led Bible study and prayer groups and taught Sunday school for many years. Also, over many years, she has written a regular article – 'Jane's Jottings' – for her parish magazine. When she contacted us, she was planning a new regular article to be part of her 'jottings', specifically for older people. She had recently received a community service award from her local parish council for her writings and wrote: 'I love writing my column and regard it as my current missionary work which I can do at home, and through which I can pass on to others some of my spiritual reading.'

No longer able to attend church due to health concerns, a home communion group meets at her home and has recently begun meeting again after the long disruptions of the pandemic.

'Being housebound,' Jane wrote, 'like so many older people in our parish I hoped I might be able, through my writings, to offer some help.'

We are delighted to include one of 'Jane's Jottings' here: her reflection for May 2022.

Jane's Jottings

March winds, April showers
Bring forth May flowers...

May is the abundant month. Its hedges are decked with hawthorn blossom while buttercups and other wildflowers adorn our meadows. And in the coming days, before Ascension Day, we celebrate Rogationtide – when by ancient custom parish boundaries are beaten and prayers are said asking for God's blessing on the crops in fields and gardens.

Practically, every fence and ditch mean a boundary of some kind, and boundaries nearly always have some historical importance. The old practice of 'beating the bounds' was a way of storing in the memory useful information when disputes arose.

In 944AD, King Edmund granted some land to a local bishop on the downs above Blewbury, south Oxfordshire. In those days, before maps, the boundaries had to be described in words. Here is part of the charter describing the estate:

'… then up to the great tumulus beneath wild garlic wood, then up along stone way to the tall crucifix at "hawk thorn tree" at Lakfield.' It is interesting to see how many 'thorns' appeared in these old documents.

I'm reading a new book by the bishop of Ramsbury, Andrew Rumsey, *English Grounds: A pastoral journal* (SCM Press, 2021), in which he follows an ancient track called The Ridgeway on the north Wiltshire downs. Pausing at The Ridgeway's intersection with Green Street, another old track, he recites Psalm 103, 'Praise the Lord O my soul: and all that is within me praise his holy Name,' taken from Rogation liturgy.

He notices that since he last walked this way the grey furrows of winter have turned into the lush soft green of a field of barley. He tells us that the walking of bounds at this season was the only outdoor religious procession to survive the English Reformation. It was not just permitted but mandated by Henry VIII and Elizabeth I.

For a thousand years these ceremonies defined the contract between God, land and humanity:

Not for ever in green pastures
do we ask our way to be;
but the steep and rugged pathway
may we tread rejoicingly.

From 'Village News for the Parishes of Calbourne, Newtown, Thorley and Shalfleet', May 2022.

Bless you!

Lin Ball

Is 'God bless you!' a greeting you use? It often comes over today as a bit soft and sentimental, a rather feeble wish. How has that happened? True blessing from God is not insipid. It's dynamic, powerful, amazing.

It is widely agreed that the sermon on the mount embodies the central principles of Christian discipleship. Religious and moral thinkers like Tolstoy and Gandhi have admired its message. While it is a call for radical living, it's entirely in step with the teaching of the prophets, especially Isaiah and Jeremiah.

With so much richness to be mined, we're going to be spending our time in the opening section – the beatitudes – which is all about how we can be blessed. We'll look at these verses in different translations – but don't worry if you haven't got all of them or can't access them online (**biblegateway.com**). In these short but memorable phrases, Jesus sets out the desirable 'heart attitudes' of the citizens of heaven, describing how believers can experience real spiritual blessing, in every situation.

It's all about the health of the heart and soul, about wholeness and human flourishing.

Matthew 5:1–3 (MSG, abridged)

You're blessed when...

When Jesus saw his ministry drawing huge crowds, he climbed a hillside. Those who were apprenticed to him, the committed, climbed with him. Arriving at a quiet place, he sat down and taught his climbing companions. This is what he said: 'You're blessed when...'

'Bless you!' is often heard in response to someone sneezing, though there's no conclusive explanation why. Theories abound. The most popular one is that in Tudor England a sneeze signified the plague and 'Bless you!' was a way of showing compassion. Yet, sneezing isn't a symptom of the plague, so it can't be that. Some think sneezing was associated with expelling a demon, which was obviously good news. But there's no evidence to support this idea, either.

So what does it mean to be 'blessed'? This word *makarios* might be translated 'fully satisfied'. Some translators use 'happy'. But it's not about any favourable or lucky circumstances you might find yourself in. Rather, it's the joyful contentment of a life captivated by the living Christ.

Jesus promises the 'good life' to those who will realign their behaviour to his ways. Is it achievable? Not perfectly. But we're invited to participate in a life of discipleship which, however flawed, shadows the footsteps of Jesus and brings us that hard-to-describe blessing as we journey.

■ **PRAYER** ·

Most merciful redeemer, friend and brother, may I know you more clearly, love you more dearly, follow you more nearly, day by day. Amen (Richard of Chichester, 1197–1253).

Matthew 5:3 (AMP)

Empty hands

'Blessed [spiritually prosperous, happy, to be admired] are the poor in spirit [those devoid of spiritual arrogance, those who regard themselves as insignificant], for theirs is the kingdom of heaven [both now and forever].'

'Blessed are the poor in spirit, for theirs is the kingdom of God.' The picture conjured up by the Greek word for 'poor in spirit' is of a beggar with nothing to offer. How can that be a blessed situation? Because it's the opposite of pride. Jesus suggests that an understanding of how little we have means that God will give to us generously.

I find this comforting. In my earlier life, it seemed easy to offer God things: my talents, my career, my commitment to the local church. But now? Now it's often my turn to be a passenger. Yes, there are things I can do. But my energy levels are lower and sometimes I need to make way for others with youth on their side. Also, the older I get, the less I think I know.

God values honest, empty hands and wants to fill them. He is attentive to those who are fully aware of their shortcomings. He has no use for pride.

■ PRAYER

Use this prayer echoing Psalm 34: Thank you, Lord, that your eyes are on me and your ears attentive to my cry; that you are close when I am broken-hearted and you save me when I am crushed in spirit. Amen

Matthew 5:4 (PHILLIPS)

Sorrow for sin

'How happy are those who know what sorrow means for they will be given courage and comfort!'

At first sight, this is an odd 'blessing': 'Blessed are those who mourn, for they will be comforted' (NIV). What kind of mourning is this? Looking at the meaning of the words used, it's clear it's about sorrow for sin. This is illustrated so beautifully in the story where Jesus is anointed by a sinful woman (Luke 7:36–50) – a woman identified by John in his gospel as Mary Magdalene. Jesus draws out the truth that the bigger the understanding of the debt cancelled, the greater the gratitude.

When I became a Christian at the age of 18, the focus of my tears was mainly on the suffering of Christ. Did such a good person really die that dreadful death? But gradually the grief switched focus to the sin in me that brought him to the cross.

We are blessed when we are genuinely sorry for our sins. Jesus said Mary 'wet my feet with her tears and wiped them with her hair… she has poured perfume on my feet.' It's a good kind of mourning.

■ **PRAYER**

Share your sorrow for sin with God and pray the words of Psalm 30: Father, 'you turned my wailing into dancing; you removed my sackcloth and clothed me with joy, that my heart may sing your praises and not be silent. Lord my God, I will praise you forever.' Amen

Matthew 5:5 (CEV)

No doormat

God blesses those people who are humble. The earth will belong to them!

If, like me, you're a baby boomer (born 1946–64), you've been raised in a culture that encourages narcissistic self-fulfilment, which doesn't serve us well as Christian disciples. Following Jesus means a different focus: 'Blessed are the meek, for they will inherit the earth' (NIV). It's unfortunate that 'meek' in our day tends to mean weak or ineffective or even easily led. That surely can't be the way to blessing?

Do you remember how remarkably God describes Moses in Numbers 12? God says Moses is the humblest person on earth. Yet Moses was also a man of great leadership skills. He was far from being a doormat: 'The Lord said… Of all my house, he is the one I trust. I speak to him face to face, clearly, and not in riddles! He sees the Lord as he is' (Numbers 12:6–8, NLT).

Another Bible version (NLV) gives Matthew 5:5 as: 'Those who have no pride in their hearts are happy.' We are blessed when we are humble before God, taking no pride in ourselves, not an act of weakness but true strength of character.

■ **PRAYER**

Lord, I long to see you clearly and closely, as Moses did. Help me to get rid of any foolish pride I have, and to know that real integrity of character and blessing lies in choosing to humbly follow you. Amen

Matthew 5:6 (PHILLIPS)

Thirsty for goodness

'Happy are those who are hungry and thirsty for goodness, for they will be fully satisfied!'

'Blessed are those who hunger and thirst for righteousness' (NIV) perhaps doesn't resonate for us as much as it did in Jesus' day, when real hunger from poverty was a more common experience.

Picture the homeless on the streets of Jerusalem – or your own nearest city – the destitute and desperate begging for food from passers-by. Then think of the urgent need to drink a glass of cool water when you've been gardening in summer, or after a long walk or cycle ride. Our hungering and thirsting for righteousness should be like that longing for a cool drink – but even more intense.

As human life is sustained with food and water, so our spiritual life is sustained with righteousness or right living. Living according to God's standards isn't possible in our own human strength. We need the help of God's Holy Spirit. Our 'right standing' before God is only possible because of Christ's sacrifice on the cross for our sins, and his Spirit living inside us.

■ **PRAYER**

Ask God to make you thirsty for righteousness. And if you are thirsty but unsatisfied, ask him for his living water to satisfy that craving. Ask him to honour the promise Jesus gave (John 7:37–38, NLT): 'Anyone who is thirsty may come to me! Anyone who believes in me may come and drink! For the Scriptures declare, "Rivers of living water will flow from his heart."' Amen

Matthew 5:7 (CEV)

Double blessing

God blesses those people who are merciful. They will be treated with mercy!

Did you study Shakespeare's *The Merchant of Venice* at school? 'The quality of mercy… droppeth as the gentle rain from heaven… It is twice blest: it blesseth him that gives and him that takes… It is an attribute to God himself.' So says Portia in a memorable passage in Act four, scene one. Mercy is a blessing to both giver and receiver.

Perhaps we can only truly show mercy to others when we have experienced forgiveness – God's mercy – ourselves. I feel that's been true of me. The rigid rule-keeping of my earlier days has, I hope, been tempered with understanding of the pressures on others as I have got older.

Mercy is something that our world desperately needs. Only mercy can counteract the misery of sin. Mercy is an essential part of God's love for the needy, the ashamed, the hurting – and it's the beginning of restoration. William Vine says that the merciful are 'not simply possessed of pity but actively compassionate.'*

■ PRAYER

Consider what impact God being 'rich in mercy' (Ephesians 2:4–7) has had on you and respond to that in prayer. Can you think of any ways in which you can show this 'attribute of God' to others more?

* William Vine, *Complete Expository Dictionary of Old and New Testament Words* (Thomas Nelson Publishers, 1985), p. 404.

Matthew 5:8 (AMP)

Pure-hearted

'Blessed [anticipating God's presence, spiritually mature] are the pure in heart [those with integrity, moral courage, and godly character], for they will see God.'

The next beatitude we come to is, 'Blessed are the pure in heart, for they will see God' (NIV). 'Pure in heart' is another way of saying 'cleansed'. The root word was often used for the process of removing impurities from precious metals. Our sin is a barrier to 'seeing' God. Only when we are clean can we stand before him at all.

Of course, we can't physically see God in this world, but those who are cleansed from sin can 'see' him at work in people and in the world. We see him present and active in his creation. We have insight or understanding into his ways. And there is another sense in which we will see God, when we are united with his returning Son Jesus, 'the image of the invisible God' (Colossians 1:15), when 'every eye will see him' (Revelation 1:7).

■ **PRAYER**

Cleanse the thoughts of my heart, Lord, by the inspiration of your Spirit. Purify me in your refining fire. I long to be holy, Lord, set apart to serve you and always ready to do your will. Amen

Matthew 5:9 (NLT)

Reconciliation

'God blesses those who work for peace, for they will be called the children of God.'

'Blessed are the peacemakers, for they will be called children of God' (NRSV). Before we belong to God, we are effectively in rebellion against his ways. When we become followers of Jesus, a peace treaty is signed and sealed. But, more than that, there is a sacred charge given to us to be peacemakers in the world. As Paul writes: 'God... gave us the ministry of reconciliation: that God was reconciling the world to himself in Christ... And he has committed to us the message of reconciliation' (2 Corinthians 5:18–19, NIV).

In other words, we are to be in the business of making peace treaties between others and God. So, how are we doing in promoting reconciliation?

I find this a daunting question... until I remind myself that the most compelling evidence of my reconciliation with God is my changed life. God simply requires me to share my changed life – my love, my joy, my hope, the things that make my life in Christ meaningful – with others, being sure to give the credit for all the good things to God and not to my own efforts.

■ PRAYER

Lord, may I be blessed for being a peacemaker. May others see what you've done in my life and be drawn to be reconciled with you. Amen

Matthew 5:10–11 (NLT)

Opposition

'God blesses those who are persecuted for doing right, for the kingdom of heaven is theirs. God blesses you when people mock you and persecute you and lie about you and say all sorts of evil things against you because you are my followers.'

It should come as no surprise to us when we face opposition undeservedly. Jesus tells us to expect it.

A vivid memory of my time as a cub reporter is of newspaper colleagues crowding and jeering around a photo of me watching an arm-waving preacher at a Salvation Army event I'd covered for the paper. The caption had been added: 'The only one to be saved...'

My embarrassment was small cost for letting my colleagues know I believed in Jesus. Opposition comes with the territory. We are out of step with the majority.

Paul encountered opposition amounting to persecution. Here's his advice: 'Whatever happens, conduct yourselves in a manner worthy of the gospel of Christ... without being frightened in any way by those who oppose you... For it has been granted to you on behalf of Christ not only to believe in him, but also to suffer for him' (Philippians 1:27–29, NIV).

■ PRAYER

'Remember my chains', writes Paul (Colossians 4:18). In many countries, Christians can face opposition of the severest kind, resulting in job loss, imprisonment or even death. Pray for your persecuted brothers and sisters to be blessed now.

Matthew 5:14–16 (NIV)

Light-giving

'You are the light of the world. A town built on a hill cannot be hidden. Neither do people light a lamp and put it under a bowl. Instead they put it on its stand, and it gives light to everyone in the house… let your light shine before others, that they may see your good deeds and glorify your Father in heaven.'

The link between light deprivation and ill health is well known. Rats kept in the dark not only exhibit depressive behaviour but also suffer brain damage. Being deprived of light has a range of bad effects on people, from disrupted sleep patterns to the onset of some chronic diseases and even cancers. We are made to live in the light.

After describing the ways in which we can be blessed, Jesus pictures his followers as salt and light – cleansing and illuminating. When we follow Jesus faithfully, we cannot help but have an impact on the people around us which will evoke a response… either they will set themselves against us or they will fall in love with the life-changing Jesus too.

The teaching of the sermon on the mount will guide us into that distinctive, holy lifestyle.

■ **PRAYER**

Father God, we see so much darkness around us. Wars, sickness, greed, envy and pride bring distress to many. As I follow Jesus, the light of the world, shine through me to give health and wholeness to others. Amen

Surprising saviours

Roger Combes

When you read a novel or a detective story, you expect surprises. There are twists in the plot that you don't expect. The villain turns out to be someone you trusted, and a vaguely suspicious character is revealed as a hero. It is the same in real life. Things happen in our lives and in the world that we would never have anticipated. Little is predictable, it seems, in life or in fiction.

The Bible tells the long history of God acting again and again to save his children. There are many surprises. God often works in unexpected ways and through unexpected saviours. We shall meet some of them in this series of reflections. Who would have thought that God would choose the unpopular Joseph, or a baby floating precariously in the bulrushes, to save the children of God? Other 'surprising saviours' were a pagan dictator, a beautiful queen, a boy who was 'too young', a bronze sculpture and a timid farmer.

It was all leading up to a carpenter from Nazareth. What could be more unlikely than a crucified saviour? It was all part of God's pattern of 'surprising saviours'.

Genesis 50:19–21 (NIV, abridged)

An unpopular brother

Joseph said to them... 'You intended to harm me, but God intended it for good to accomplish what is now being done, the saving of many lives. So then, don't be afraid. I will provide for you and your children.' And he reassured them and spoke kindly to them.

Did you grow up with a younger brother? Did you fight with him? Did you ever hit him or treat him badly? Joseph had ten older brothers who should have known better when they overpowered him, aged 17, and put him in a pit to kill him. In the event, they 'merely' sold the terrified youngster to some slave traders. Then they took the money and ran.

Imagine how they felt when, 20 years later, they came face to face with him again. A severe famine was sweeping through the region, and the one person who could save them happened to be the young brother they had once disposed of so cruelly. Now *he* had the power of life and death over them. They were shocked and afraid.

It was all part of God's providence. Joseph did save his brothers and their families, as the Lord intended. Joseph said he would provide for them, and completely forgive them for the way they had treated him. Now they had to believe it.

■ **PRAYER**

Thank you, Lord, for our saviour, who, like Joseph, has saved his brothers and sisters though they have sinned against him. Amen

Exodus 2:5–6, 10 (NIV, abridged)

A baby in the bulrushes

Pharaoh's daughter went down to the Nile to bathe… She saw the basket among the reeds and sent her female slave to get it. She opened it and saw the baby. He was crying and she felt sorry for him. 'This is one of the Hebrew babies,' she said… She named him Moses, saying, 'I drew him out of the water.'

Cruise ships have been carrying tourists on the Nile for over a century. Over 3,000 years before, baby Moses was found in the shallows of the same great African river, floating in a basket. A princess who found him took pity on him and, despite her father's decree that all Hebrew baby boys should die, she resolved to raise Moses herself. She took him home to the palace, and there he would grow up with the best education and training in the land. Of course, God was in it all.

This vulnerable baby should, by law, have died. But his midwives defied the instructions to kill him, his resourceful mother hatched a risky plan – did his father craft a waterproof basket I wonder? – and the princess had a kind heart. He survived.

The Hebrew slaves making their bricks had no idea that their rescuer and future leader was a foster child growing up in the palace.

■ **PRAYER**

Heavenly Father, through Moses you brought your people out of Egypt. Help parents in harsh conditions, especially oppressed peoples, as they bring their children into adulthood. Amen

Numbers 21:8–9 (NIV)

A bronze sculpture

The Lord said to Moses, 'Make a snake and put it on a pole; anyone who is bitten can look at it and live.' So Moses made a bronze snake and put it up on a pole. Then when anyone was bitten by a snake and looked at the bronze snake, they lived.

We were walking in the Drakensberg mountains in South Africa. The beauty was breathtaking. I had never seen anywhere like it. Then, just ahead, came squeals of fear, and I saw a small deadly snake beside the path. No one was hurt, but my heart beat a bit faster.

When the children of Israel were experiencing life-threatening snake bites in the desert, the Lord provided an unlikely cure. The only remedy for someone who had been bitten was to look at a bronze model of a snake that had been erected in the camp. They did not have to touch it or move close to it – just *look* at it. And it worked. They recovered and lived.

'Look to me, and be saved, all ends of the earth you!' (Isaiah 45:22, NKJV) was the verse that brought Charles Haddon Spurgeon, the great Baptist leader, to grasp the gospel. 'A life for a look at the Saviour!' he exclaimed. Anyone, anywhere, in any need can do it. Looking to the Saviour brings eternal life.

■ PRAYER

Praise God for his provision of a saviour, lifted up on a cross, for us to turn to.

Judges 6:12, 14–16 (NIV, abridged)

A timid farmer

When the Lord appeared to Gideon, he said, 'The Lord is with you, mighty warrior… Go in the strength you have and save Israel out of Midian's hand. Am I not sending you?'… Gideon replied, 'But how can I save Israel? My clan is the weakest in Manasseh, and I am the least in my family.' The Lord answered, 'I will be with you.'

The humble bee seems so insignificant, flitting from flower to flower. Yet it is a major global pollinator and without it we would run out of food. The unseen earthworm is indispensable as it burrows in our soil to make it fertile. Underwater, fragile coral grows to support thousands of exquisite marine species.

Gideon saw himself as insignificant and weak. Perhaps he was shy or diffident, or perhaps just modest and retiring. Later, he was scared of the reaction of the townspeople and his family. We might think him an unlikely person to save God's people from Midianite invaders ravaging their farms. But God chose him.

Gideon and only 100 men were able to strike terror into an entire Midianite-Amalekite army and put them to flight. Gideon believed the Lord who was sending him, and the Lord would go with him. He was a mighty warrior after all.

■ PRAYER

Lord, when the task you give me is daunting or everything threatens to overwhelm me, please take away my fears and give me the confidence to tackle the future for you and with you. Amen

1 Samuel 17:32–33, 50 (GNT)

A young shepherd

David said to Saul, 'Your Majesty, no one should be afraid of this Philistine! I will go and fight him.' 'No,' answered Saul. 'How could you fight him? You're just a boy, and he has been a soldier all his life!'... And so, without a sword, David defeated and killed Goliath with a sling and a stone!

'You're just a boy!' said the king. David was probably in his teens in this story. Do you have memories of being dismissed by older people just because of your youth? Were they being sensible or overprotective? Or were they simply lacking the imagination to see you succeeding? Age and experience aren't necessary for every responsibility. Prodigious young musicians and athletes triumph and delight crowds all the time.

The young David was an expert in protecting his sheep from predators, and these skills were transferable. He smartly dispatched Goliath, the Philistine champion. Who could have guessed? What a turnaround for the Israelites and King Saul. The Philistine army fled, and the Israelite army pursued. All the people rejoiced and entered into David's victory, just as we rejoice and enter into the victory won eternally for us by the Lord Jesus when he was only 33.

■ **PRAYER**

Pray for those with heavy responsibilities on young shoulders: young carers, for example, who come home from school every day to care for a disabled parent or sibling; or young men and women in the Armed Forces, risking their own safety to protect others.

Jeremiah 38:6–10 (NIV, abridged)

An obscure civil servant

They lowered Jeremiah by ropes into the cistern… and Jeremiah sank down into the mud. But Ebed-Melek, a Cushite, an official in the royal palace… said to [the king], 'My lord the king, these men have acted wickedly'… The king commanded Ebed-Melek the Cushite, 'Take thirty men from here with you and lift Jeremiah the prophet out of the cistern before he dies.'

Dial 999! Fire, ambulance, police or coastguard services will respond all over the UK. Whatever the emergency, highly trained professionals will come and take the best course of action. In my experience, paramedics are exemplary: sensible, skilled and caring. In an emergency, you need someone who knows what to do.

God's prophet, Jeremiah, had an emergency. His enemies had imprisoned him on a false charge and forced him into a cistern, where he would soon die if nothing was done. Jerusalem was under siege and the king was too weak to act. But working somewhere in the palace was Ebed-Melek, an African from present-day Sudan. He immediately sought out the king and secured permission to stage a rescue.

His swift initiative saved Jeremiah's life. When Jerusalem eventually fell, the Lord specifically protected Ebed-Melek from death and capture (Jeremiah 39:15–18). We never know how many servants the Lord has behind the scenes, trusting him and ready to respond when the need arises. Perhaps we are one of them.

■ PRAYER

Lord, when others are in need, may my response be timely, practical and caring. Amen

2 Chronicles 36:22b–23 (NIV, abridged)

A foreign dictator

The Lord moved the heart of Cyrus king of Persia to make a proclamation… 'The Lord, the God of heaven, has given me all the kingdoms of the earth and he has appointed me to build a temple for him at Jerusalem in Judah. Any of his people among you may go up, and may the Lord their God be with them.'

My mother used to listen to every news bulletin 'in case something has happened'. But if I asked her what was on the news, she would say, 'Nothing much.' The news can be dull and depressing. It can make us feel powerless, as if the world is run by a few powerful people and we are helpless to do anything about it.

The Jews in Babylon probably felt like that. Successive kings of Babylon had held them captive for decades. Their policy would not change. Then, Cyrus, a king of Persia, invaded and conquered Babylon in 539BC. Within a year, everything was different. He was more sympathetic to the captured peoples of his new land. He decreed that they could worship their own gods, and Jews could return and rebuild their temple in Jerusalem. This pagan ruler was God's instrument for setting his people free (see Isaiah 44:24-45:13). Here is the news. God 'moved the heart' of Cyrus the king. He still rules over the hearts and decisions of those who run our world.

■ **PRAYER**
Pray for those who are in positions of power in the world.

Esther 7:2–4 (NIV, abridged)

A beauty contest queen

[King Xerxes] again asked, 'Queen Esther, what is your petition? It will be given you. What is your request?'… Queen Esther answered, 'If I have found favour with you, Your Majesty, and if it pleases you, grant me my life – this is my petition. And spare my people – this is my request. For I and my people have been sold to be destroyed, killed and annihilated.'

The Persian empire, stretching from Egypt to India, was run by men. Women had little say. King Xerxes, who ruled 486–465BC, did not even allow the queen to approach him without his permission, on pain of death. When he wanted a new queen, he organised a beauty contest, which was won by Esther, a local orphan.

Later, all Jews across the empire were about to be massacred following a new decree from the king. Their prospect was bleak. They had no spokesman. Esther, the young queen, had told no one she was Jewish. But she was brave. She put her own life on the line and approached the king. Xerxes listened. He rescinded the decree and punished its author. Large numbers of Jews across the Middle East owed their lives to Esther. Their saviour, unlikely in the circumstances, was a woman, an orphan, Jewish and the king's favourite. Ask yourself whether, despite the restrictions you face, you may still be well-placed to improve someone else's life.

■ **PRAYER**

Pray for all those who feel marginalised or mistreated in the country where they live. Pray for all who combat antisemitism and racism.

Matthew 1:20b–21 (NIV)

A surprise baby

An angel of the Lord appeared to [Joseph] in a dream and said, 'Joseph son of David, do not be afraid to take Mary home as your wife, because what is conceived in her is from the Holy Spirit. She will give birth to a son, and you are to give him the name Jesus, because he will save his people from their sins.'

'A baby? You?' What a shock for Joseph. Imagine what was going through his mind after Mary broke the news to him. He was now engaged to a pregnant young woman who insisted she was a virgin. What would the family think? How was he to face the respectable Jewish neighbourhood? Indeed, how could he face God? Should he call the wedding off?

The Lord sent an angel specially to Joseph to reassure him. Mary's baby was of God, no less. He would be Jesus, the conqueror of the world's evil, who 'will save his people from their sins'.

Years later, there were others puzzled about Jesus, saying, 'Nazareth! Can anything good come from there?' (John 1:46) and 'Isn't this the carpenter?' (Mark 6:3). Even today, we sometimes ignore Jesus because he does not fit in with our ideas of what God would do. But Joseph took it all in. He married and supported Mary, becoming the committed earthly father of the Saviour of the world.

■ PRAYER
Lord Jesus Christ, you are full of surprises, and a greater saviour than I could ever imagine. Amen

Matthew 27:39–42 (NRSV, abridged)

A man on a cross

Those who passed by derided him, shaking their heads and saying... 'If you are the Son of God, come down from the cross.' In the same way the chief priests also, along with the scribes and elders, were mocking him, saying, 'He saved others; he cannot save himself... Let him come down from the cross now, and we will believe in him.'

In the French Revolution, some spectators sat knitting as they watched the public executions. Today, onlookers outside a court will sometimes jeer angrily as an accused person arrives to face charges.

As Jesus was hanging on the cross, passers-by poked fun at him, joking that he was not much of a saviour if he could not save himself. Other cruel banter followed. 'How could he be God's son,' the argument went, 'if God lets him die like a criminal?' How could a dying Jesus be the Messiah of the living God? But he was, and he is. It is precisely *because* he died on the cross that he was the sacrifice for our sin and we know how much he loves us. His death and resurrection have opened the gate of glory to welcome us home.

■ **PRAYER**

Suffering anguish, despised and rejected,
bearing our sins, my redeemer is he!

Living, he loved me; dying, he saved me;
buried, he carried my sins far away;
rising, he justified freely forever,
one day he's coming: O glorious day!'

'One day!' by J. Wilbur Chapman (1859–1918)

Fruit that lasts

I no longer call you servants, because a servant does not know his master's business. Instead, I have called you friends, for everything that I learned from my Father I have made known to you. You did not choose me, but I chose you and appointed you so that you might go and bear fruit – fruit that will last – and so that whatever you ask in my name the Father will give you.

JOHN 15:15–16 (NIV)

In this verse Jesus is speaking to his disciples in the upper room, giving them a farewell and a sending out, words of comfort and empowerment to get them through the coming days. Here he makes it explicit, those gathered in the room are his friends. Their relationship has transcended that of master and servant through the sharing of knowledge. For a servant simply follows the orders of the master, while a friend with profound understanding can take initiative and carry ideas forward – and ultimately bear lasting fruit.

For over 100 years, BRF has been working to share the knowledge of the gospel with as many people of all ages as possible, whether through our Bible reading notes, like those you are now holding, or the wider work of our ministries – Anna Chaplaincy, Living Faith, Messy Church and Parenting for Faith. It is our goal not only to share the Bible but also to give people the tools for building a deeper understanding of and a closer friendship with God, which will then bear fruit in their own lives and in their communities.

Our work is made possible through kind donations from individuals, charitable trusts and gifts in wills. If you would like to support BRF's work you can become a Friend of BRF by making a monthly gift of £2 a month or more – we thank you for your friendship.

Find out more at **brf.org.uk/donate**.

Judith Moore
Fundraising development officer

Across a year's worth of weekly reflections, Gordon Giles focuses on objects, scenes, activities and places, drawing out spiritual insights to help us reflect on what we have learned as we venture out again after months of restriction, absence and anxiety. We consider: What is it like spiritually to stop wearing masks? What does a beach say to us after coronavirus? How has Zoom affected us during lockdown and how do we now relate to technology as a medium of fellowship? Where is Christ amid our restrictions and our releases?

At Home and Out and About
52 biblical contemplations on faith, hope and love for a re-emerging world
Gordon Giles
978 1 80039 115 4 £9.99
brfonline.org.uk

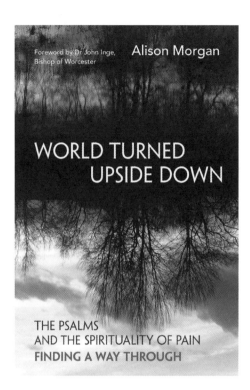

There are no simple answers to life's challenges, so how do we integrate our most testing experiences into our faith in a way which strengthens rather than weakens it? With the psalmists as our guides, we learn to draw closer to God, to hear his voice in fresh ways, and to identify what it is that troubles us. Borrowing their words, we find that we are able to articulate our most painful feelings and walk through suffering with honesty, hope, and confidence in the God who travels beside us. Here is an opportunity to read the Psalms differently: an invitation to embark on a new journey.

World Turned Upside Down
The Psalms and the spirituality of pain
Alison Morgan
978 1 80039 166 6 £12.99
brfonline.org.uk

To order

Online: **brfonline.org.uk**
Telephone: +44 (0)1865 319700
Mon–Fri 9.30–17.00
Post: complete this form and send to the address below

Delivery times within the UK are
normally 15 working days. Prices are
correct at the time of going to press
but may change without prior notice.

Title	Issue	Price	Qty	Total
At Home and Out and About		£9.99		
World Turned Upside Down		£12.99		
Bible Reflections for Older People (single copy)	May–Aug 2023	£5.50		
Bible Reflections for Older People (single copy)	Sep–Dec 2023	£5.50		

POSTAGE AND PACKING CHARGES			
Order value	UK	Europe	Rest of world
Under £7.00	£2.00		
£7.00–£29.99	£3.00	Available on request	Available on request
£30.00 and over	FREE		

Total value of books	
Donation	
Postage and packing	
Total for this order	

Please complete in BLOCK CAPITALS

Title .... First name/initials .... Surname...

Address ....

.... Postcode ....

Acc. No. .... Telephone ....

Email ....

Method of payment

❑ Cheque (made payable to BRF) ❑ MasterCard / Visa

Card no. [ ][ ][ ][ ] [ ][ ][ ][ ] [ ][ ][ ][ ] [ ][ ][ ][ ]

Expires end [M][M] [Y][Y] Security code [ ][ ][ ] Last 3 digits on the reverse of the card

We will use your personal data to process this order. From
time to time we may send you information about the work
of BRF. Please contact us if you wish to discuss your mailing
preferences **brf.org.uk/privacy**

Registered with
FUNDRAISING REGULATOR

Please return this form to:

BRF, 15 The Chambers, Vineyard, Abingdon OX14 3FE | **enquiries@brf.org.uk**
For terms and cancellation information, please visit brfonline.org.uk/terms.

Bible Reading Fellowship (BRF) is a charity (233280) and company limited by guarantee (301324),
registered in England and Wales

BIBLE REFLECTIONS FOR OLDER PEOPLE **GROUP SUBSCRIPTION FORM**

All our Bible reading notes can be ordered online
by visiting **brfonline.org.uk/subscriptions**

The group subscription rate for *Bible Reflections for Older People* will be £16.50 per person until April 2024.

☐ I would like to take out a group subscription for .... (*quantity*) copies.

☐ Please start my order with the September 2023 / January 2024 / May 2024* issue.
(*delete as appropriate*)

Please do not send any money with your order. Send your order to BRF and we will send you an invoice.

Name and address of the person organising the group subscription:

Title .... First name/initials .... Surname ....

Address ....

.... Postcode ....

Telephone .... Email ....

Church ....

Name and address of the person paying the invoice if the invoice needs to be sent directly to them:

Title .... First name/initials .... Surname ....

Address ....

.... Postcode ....

Telephone .... Email ....

Please return this form to:
BRF, 15 The Chambers, Vineyard, Abingdon OX14 3FE | **enquiries@brf.org.uk**
For terms and cancellation information, please visit brfonline.org.uk/terms.

Bible Reading Fellowship is a charity (233280) and company limited by guarantee (301324),
registered in England and Wales

BROP0223

BIBLE REFLECTIONS FOR OLDER PEOPLE INDIVIDUAL/GIFT SUBSCRIPTION FORM

> To order online, please visit **brfonline.org.uk/subscriptions**

☐ I would like to take out a subscription (*complete your name and address details only once*)
☐ I would like to give a gift subscription (*please provide both names and addresses*)

Title .... First name/initials .... Surname ....

Address ....

.... Postcode ....

Telephone .... Email ....

Gift subscription name ....

Gift subscription address ....

.... Postcode ....

Gift message (*20 words max. or include your own gift card*):

....

....

Please send *Bible Reflections for Older People* beginning with the September 2023 / January 2024 / May 2024* issue (*delete as appropriate*):

(*please tick box*)	UK	Europe	Rest of world
Bible Reflections for Older People	☐ £20.85	☐ £28.05	☐ £32.10

Total enclosed £ .... (*cheques should be made payable to 'BRF'*)

Please charge my MasterCard / Visa with £ ....

Card no. ☐☐☐☐ ☐☐☐☐ ☐☐☐☐ ☐☐☐☐

Expires end ☐☐☐☐   Security code ☐☐☐   Last 3 digits on the reverse of the card

We will use your personal data to process this order. From time to time we may send you information about the work of BRF. Please contact us if you wish to discuss your mailing preferences **brf.org.uk/privacy**

Please return this form to:
BRF, 15 The Chambers, Vineyard, Abingdon OX14 3FE | **enquiries@brf.org.uk**
For terms and cancellation information, please visit brfonline.org.uk/terms.

Bible Reading Fellowship is a charity (233280) and company limited by guarantee (301324), registered in England and Wales